SWEET POTATO PRODUCTION [BASIC]

GOALS OF THIS BOOKLET

This booklet was designed and written to educate its' readers on the growing and storage of sweet potatoes *'ipomea batatas'*. In it you will find knowledge on:

- Nutritional value of sweet potatoes,
- Land preparation and fumigants, pesticides and herbicides to use,
- Vine lengths and planting orientations for maximum growth and yields,
- Suitable soil types,
- Correct fertilisers and nutrient quantities,
- Sustainable irrigation method and appropriate water quantities [see Appendices B -G for crop water requirements],
- Diseases [viruses and weevils] which affect tubers together with their control.

This book can be used as a manual or as a reference for both domestic and commercial production of sweet potatoes. In it you will also find some traditional technologies of storing this precious tuber. The contents of this book are well researched to the best knowledge of the author.

List of Abbreviations

AREX	Ministry of Lands and Agriculture, Department of Agricultural Research and Extension
CIAT	International Center for Tropical Agriculture
CWR	Crop Water Requirement
HRI	Horticultural Research Institute
NDJ	NaanDanJain
RH	Relative Humidity
SADC	Southern Africa Development Community
SARRNET	Southern Africa Root Crops Research Network

List of Tables

List of Figures

List of Appendices

Table of Contents

Sweet Potato

Sweet potato '*ipomea batatas*' comes in many varieties and colours, ranging from cream-coloured varieties to the deep orange ones and purple ones. The flesh of the dark orange sweet potatoes tends to be sweeter and creamier than that of the pale yellow ones or the purple ones, which resemble the drier, starchier flesh of a russet potato [Filippone, 2017]. Some of the sweet potato varieties are shown in Figure 1 and most of the ones common in Zimbabwe are shown in Table 1.

Nutritional Value

Sweet potato is ranked highest in nutritional value amongst other root crops. It is fat-free and contains beta carotenes, vitamins [A, C and E], magnesium, potassium and antioxidants [Dukuh, I. G. *et al*, 2015]. A medium sweet potato contains daily required nutrients of 4% iron, 35% vitamin C and 4 times vitamin A [NCSPC, 2018]. WFLO [2008], shows that sweet potatoes contain the following thermal properties as percentages, moisture 72.84 %, protein 1.65 %, fat 0.30 %, carbohydrate 24.28 %, fibre 3 % and ash 0.95 %.

Figure 1: Different types of Sweet potatoes with different matter colours [Google Images, 17 May 2018]

Sweet potato are less affected by price rise and fall than most of the main cereals as they are not regionally or internationally traded crops [Sanginga, N, 2015]. Its' production can be up to 50 t/ha [Coertze & Van de Berg, 1995, cited by Parwada *et al*, 2011].

Sweet Potato Varieties in Zimbabwe

Sweet potato varieties common in Zimbabwe, according to Horticultural Research Institute [HRI] in Marondera as shown in Table 1. These are found in different market places across the country, Mbare, Bulawayo, Gweru and others. Sweet potatoes are grown in most parts of the country [Zimbabwe], but the main production zones are found in Mashonaland Central, Mashonaland East, Mashonaland West, Manicaland, Masvingo, and Midlands [AREX, 2004].

Table 1: Showing sweet potato varieties common in Zimbabwe.

VARIETY	QUALITIES		
	Description [General]	Maturity Period [months]	Yield [tonnes/ha]
Chingovha [SPN/O]	Cream skin & flesh Long starchy tubes, which stores well	3-4	25
Germany Two	Red skinned & white flesh Starchy & sweet long tube	3-4	30
Mozambique White	Red skinned & white flesh Average sized tubes, which are smooth skinned Most favored in supermarkets'	6	35
Brondal	Light red skin & cream flesh Cylindrical big tubes, which are easy to lift Commonly Processed into chip & flour	4-5 [135 days [Parwada *et al*, 2011]]	31-35
Cordner	Bronze coloured skin and orange fleshed Chunky tubers which are rich in carotene	------	30
Magutse	Khaki skin & light cream flesh	4-5	50
Pamhai	Pale skin & cream flesh, long thick tube	-------	30
Mafutha	Dirty skin & cream flesh, large tubes	4	20-30

Land Preparation & Planting

Land preparation

Sweet potatoes generally do well in loamy soils and clays that allow for easy growth of the tubers. Ideal temperatures range from 18-27°C [Mutandwa, 2008]. These soils should be well drained. While this crop can be grown in heavier soils, roots may be rough-skinned and irregular as a result. Fields high in organic matter should be avoided. Sweet potatoes should not be grown on the same land more often than once every 3 years. Avoid fields with a history of difficult to control perennial weeds [Kaiser & Ernst, 2014].

In Zimbabwe, with respect to natural regions [see Appendices A], the crop is produced mainly in agro-ecological Zones I, II, and III. Natural Region I covers most parts of Manicaland province [Mutare & Chipinge], Natural Region II covers part of Mashonaland Central, Mashonaland East, Mashonaland West, and Manicaland Provinces [Bindura, Marondera, Chinhoyi, Chegutu, and Rusape]. Natural Region III has very erratic rainfall of less than 500 mm per annum [Rukuni & Eicher, 2006] and generally spans across the Midlands province [Kwekwe, Gweru, and Kadoma].

Ridge size and spacing

Sweet potatoes do much better on sandier soils [Windmill, 2014], but also tolerates a wide range of soils including acidic. Soil pH should be adjusted to about 6.0 by applying lime or dolomite. Rates of 240 kg and 400 kg/ha respectively will raise the pH by 0.1 of a unit [New Farmer Zimbabwe, 2014]. They favour areas with relatively high rainfall but cannot withstand water logging, hence they are grown on ridges and mounds of which land is ploughed to a depth of 0.3 m, with ridges 0.5 m wide with a height of 0.3-0.4 m [Parwada *et al*, 2011]. The soil should be deep ripped and then disk cultivate to break up any large clods and provide loose soil for hilling of beds.

Planting

Planting period

Planting time is mainly determined by the climate of a location. Sweet potato plants are damaged by light frost and the plants require high temperatures for a period of 4-5 months to yield well. In areas with mild frost, mid-November to mid-December is the best time to plant, and usually the crops get ready for harvest from April to May. It's common to plant from January to March in frost free areas so that the growing season extends through winter. Cold spells during winter can be a risk depending on the climate of the specific area. In very hot areas, planting should be avoided from November to middle of February as storage root formation is reduced by high temperatures [New Farmer Zimbabwe, 2014].

Propagation and Seedbed production of cuttings

Sweet Potatoes are propagated from sprouts or from slips [vine cuttings]; sprouts are preferred. Sprouts are grown from plant stock selected for its appearance, freedom from disease and off-types. Approximately 75 kg of planting stock sweet potatoes are needed to produce enough sprouts to plant one hectare. This involves the propagation of cuttings from harvested roots which are placed together in a seedbed. This is an alternative method of producing plant material which requires less labour but does sacrifice a percentage of marketable roots as shown in Figure 2 [New Farmer Zimbabwe, 2014].

Sprout production

Sprouts are produced from the conditioned roots in cold frames, heated beds, or field beds of clean sand or fumigated sandy soils. Conditioned roots are covered by soil sand, though not too much. 4-5 weeks are needed to develop strong plants when soil has been kept at 23-26 °C. 6-8 weeks may be needed if roots have not been "pre conditioned". Adequate moisture is especially critical to germination of the sprouts and proper root formation on the sprouts [New Farmer Zimbabwe, 2014].

Vine size and spacing

Parwada *et al*, 2011, encourages that vines are cut into 0.3 m long and planted with two thirds of their lengths [0.2 m] buried into the soil uniformly. Vine space of 0.3 m can be used, while making sure equal number of nodes are buried in the soil. Windmill [2014] suggests a spacing of 1.0 - 1.5 m between the rows and 0.25 – 0.6 m within the row, depending on variety and location. When it comes to vines used for new crop propagation, Windmill [2014] suggests vine sections of 0.3-0.4 m, which are disease/ virus free. Cuttings need to be watered at or immediately after planting.

Tip cutting should be taken from crops that are old enough to provide material without excessive damage. Avoid "back cuts" as these will have variable maturity and result in significant yield reduction. The lower leaves should be cut away as tearing these off may damage the nodes that will produce the roots. Cuttings can be left under a moist cloth in the shade for a couple of days to promote nodal rooting before planting in the field. Plantings should be scheduled to allow for progressive fortnightly harvest over the desired production period [New Farmer Zimbabwe, 2014].

Figure 3: Vine propagation & planting under plastic mulch [Google images, 17 May 2018].

Vine orientation

Sweet potato roots grow downwards following positive geotropism therefore vines are planted horizontally. This orientation promotes roots that are evenly spaced allowing them a larger area from which to tap water and nutrients from, thereby promoting high vine growth, thicker roots and high yields [Parwada *et al*, 2011]. This crop does not like cold or wet conditions, therefore plant out as early as possible after danger of frost is past. Crop requires 120 frost free days to maturity [Windmill, 2014].

Mulch

Plastic mulch can be used as it yields to earlier production, greater yields, and higher quality [Lamont W, 2014]. Black mulch can result in 2-14 days earlier harvest while clear mulch can result in a 21-day earlier harvest [Sanders D, 2001]. Lamont [2014] shows that Black mulch is ideal for production as it prevents weed growth by prohibiting light transmittance to the soil were as a clear plastic mulch has the highest soil warming capability, but weed growth underneath can be extreme, in Figure 3 [New England Vegetable Guide, n.d].

It has to be noted that the use of plastic mulch without trickle irrigation is not recommended, especially on very light textured [sandy] soils that has very little water holding capacity. This is so as plastic mulch prevent normal precipitation from penetrating through to the crop where it may be needed most, therefore trickle irrigation will ensure that the crop will get the needed moisture at critical periods that is flowering, fruit set and maturity [Fritz VA, 2012].

Fumigation, Fertigation & Irrigation

Fumigation

When doing seedbeds for slips, first fumigate the site before planting out roots, close together but not touching. 400 kg to get enough slips for 1 ha land [Windmill, 2014]. Directions and fumigants to use are shown in Table 2. Windmill [2014], suggest the following Pesticide and herbicides for sweet potato production together with quantities to use when dealing with pests and weeds as shown in Table 3.

Table 2: Fumigants for Eelworm on seedbed.

Problem	Product	Application Rate	Application/Comment	Rate/100 m²
Eelworm	Basamid Granules	50 g/m²	Broadcast over bed & incorporate to 0.15 m depth & cover with plastic sheet for 10-14 days	5 kg
	EDB Tech	275 mℓ / 100 m row	Tine application in rows 38 cm apart	725 mℓ

Table 3: Pesticides and Herbicides used in sweet potato production.

Problem	Product	Application Rate	Application/Comment	Rate / 1 ha
Eelworm	EDB Tech	125 mℓ / 100 m row	Or 3ml / planting station OR good rotations.	11 ℓ
Grasses	Agil 100 EC	30 mℓ /15 ℓ knapsack	Post emergent on grasses only	0.5 ℓ
Leaf eaters	Carbaryl 85WP	30 g /15 ℓ knapsack	Full cover spray. Add 5% molasses	0.5 kg
Weevils	Can do a lot of damage mainly in heavier soils		Best control is hygiene and good rotations	
			Destroy any residual plants after harvesting	

Fertigation

The sweet potato responds well to fertilisation and fertile soil. In soils with inadequate phosphorus and potassium, a high level of fertilisation is required before planting, and a steady supply of nitrogen is required throughout the growing season [NDJ, 2014].

Decomposed cattle manure can be broadcasted at a rate of 20 t/ha and incorporated into the soil [Parwada *et al*, 2011]. Too much nitrogen applied too early can lead to excessive vegetative growth, therefore select a fertiliser that contains Boron [Windmill, 2014]. Windmill [2014], suggests the following as base and top dressing as shown in Table 4, on basal application either compound C or D can be used. When using soluble fertilisers, chemicals can be incorporated in irrigation water through drip irrigation.

Table 4: Fertiliser Requirements [Windmill, 2014]

Fertiliser		Product	N %	P %	K %	S %	Rate/ha	Comment
Base Dressing	Compound C	5:15:12 11S 0.1B	15	45	36	33	300 kg	All at planting
	Compound D	4:17:11 8.5S 0.25B	12	51	33	26	300 kg	All at planting
Top Dressing	AN	AN [34.5 %]	35				100 kg	In 3-4 weeks

Irrigation

According to Bradley A. King and Jeffrey C. Stark [1997], the water sensitive nature of potatoes, combined with its shallow root zone, favors irrigation systems that are capable of light, frequent, and uniform water applications.[1] In light with this Drip irrigation on potatoes has proved to make yield increases, quality improvements, ease of field accessibility and a reduction in water, fuel, labour and fungicide use [The Toro Company, 2010]. Production through surface drip is shown in Figure 4, but subsurface drip can also be used.

Drip

The first irrigation of the season establishes the wetting pattern and can be longer than subsequent irrigations usually 24 hours, or 48 hours in dry years. During each irrigation, wetting pattern needs to effectively rewet the root zone. Fine particles or salts in the soil can be moved laterally with the initial wetting front, and they stop moving when the water ceases to move outward. Water field more frequently as less water is applied per irrigation and also, moisture may be wicked away from the root zone as the irrigated soil and surrounding dry soil equilibrate [Anon, n.d]. For proper irrigation scheduling refer to Appendices B to Appendices G .

Surface drip

The best position to align drip tape is when sweet potato seeds or vines are planted directly in line with the drip tape, these propagation material will be in the best irrigated part of the soil [Shock CC. *et al*, 2013]. When using drip, water applied at any one irrigation should not exceed the soil's water-holding capacity.

---

[1] Using these criteria as a basis for ranking the suitability of common irrigation methods, the order of preference from highest to lowest would be: drip, solid-set [portable], linear-move, centre-pivot, side-roll, hand-move, and furrow.

Figure 4: Sweet potatoes produced via surface drip irrigation [Google Images 15 May 2018]

Subsurface drip

Subsurface drip system is used to provide water to plant roots while maintaining a relatively dry soil surface, which ensures that applied water becomes available to a substantial fraction of the plant root system [Badr *et al,* 2012]. It can be used to apply water in small amounts and achieve water savings in comparison to surface drip irrigation in sandy loam textured soil. The drip tape is commonly installed within a depth of 10-30 cm below the soil surface [Patel & Rajput, 2008].

The use of subsurface drip offers many other advantages for crop production, including less nutrients leaching compared to surface irrigation, higher yields, a dry soil surface for improved weed control and crop health and the ability to apply water and nutrients to the most active part of the root zone [Patel & Rajput, 2007].

Harvesting, Storage & Marketing

Harvesting

Harvesting equipment

Plough or potato harvester may be used but cause damage so forks or spades are more advantageous [FAO, n.d]. During harvesting physical damage can occur to tubers, either damaged by mechanical force during harvest, handling and transportation, leading to physical loses [Hall AJ and Devereau D, 2000].

Harvesting damages

Cuts, bruising, and skinning are physical damages to tubers that can be minimised by careful handling and storing in boxes and cartons instead of cloth sacks. Striking the roots with harvesting equipment or dropping them into containers injures their skin. The sweet potato may be cut or bruised if they are placed in containers having sharp edges or roughly hauled or handled [Sumner P.E. 1984].

Storage

Pretreatment of sweet potato

Sweet potatoes are highly perishable food source that are susceptible to destruction by microorganisms, metabolic spoilage, physical destruction and pests [Devereau AD. 1994]. They have proved to be difficult to store for extended periods of time [Karuri, E.G. and Ojijo, N.K.O. 1994], mainly due to the fact that they have a high moisture content, thin, permeable skin and metabolic activity following harvesting [Devereau AD. 1994]. Following harvest, sweet potatoes are susceptible to spoilage by physical, physiological, pathological, pests and environmental means as shown in Figure 5. Typically sweet potatoes are stored and eaten fresh [Mutandwa E, and Gadzirayi CT. 2007].

Pretreatment of sweet potato can help to minimise risk of losses as curing can toughen the skin and heal minor physical damages while drying can reduce spoilage and inactivate metabolic degradation [Devereau AD. 1994]. It prevents against excessive moisture loss, entry of microorganisms into the tubers [Ewell, P. 1993, Kapinga RE *et al,* 2003]. Drying and curing of sweet potatoes are two common methods used to prepare them prior to storage and has proved to increase their storability and helps to minimise risk of losses [Karuri, E.G. and Hagenimana, V. 1995].

Drying [Small scale production]

Drying of tubers is mainly used in small scale production. This method is done on sweet potatoes that are too damaged to be stored fresh but still have edible material on them. Drying removes moisture, reduces bacterial growth, and inactivates metabolic processes and enzymatic decomposition [Devereau AD. 1994]. This method involves slicing tubers to a thickness of approximately 2-4 mm and then laying them out in the sun for four days or until they are rid of most of their moisture. Dried slices are kept in-doors or in raised silos until eaten. Another way of drying is to wrap tubers in black polythene sheets and leave out in the sun for 5 days. The black sheet keeps moisture in and collects heat to reach necessary conditions for curing.

Curing [Commercial/Large scale production]

Curing is done by exposing the whole potatoes to a moderately high temperature for several days immediately following harvest. Temperatures of 30-32 °C and RH 80–95% for 4-10 days has been found to be adequate curing conditions [Devereau AD. 1994]. The curing room should allow sufficient exchange of air to prevent the accumulation of CO_2 produced by the roots or depletion of O_2 consumed by them. If condensation is excessive, it is removed by ventilation. [Sumner P.E. 1984]. Immediately following curing the temperature must be dropped quickly in order to avoid sprouting damage.

Ideal storage conditions

Tubers that have been mechanically damaged, infected with pests or pathogens, or are rotten or sprouting should not be kept [Ramirez P, 1992]. Undamaged sweet potatoes can be stored for a period of 4-6 months in temperatures of 12-15°C or left in the soil if its' very dry until required [windmill, 2014]. Devereau AD [1994], notes that optimum storage of sweet potatoes occurs at 12–16 °C, 85–90% relative humidity [RH] but requires proper ventilation to remove excess CO_2 [CO_2 increases the spoilage rate] and bring in oxygen [O_2] for respiration.[2] Some of the spoilage factors are highlighted in Figure 5.

---

[2] Sweet potatoes can convert approximately 57 dm^3 of O_2/ton/day to CO_2 and need ventilation to compensate for this. The O_2 in the storage environment should not fall below 7% and CO_2 must not exceed 10% [Devereau AD, 1994]. At these conditions sweet potatoes have been shown to last 5 months to a maximum of a year compared to 2-3 months normally.

Figure 5: Sweet potato spoilage factors [L. Kaunda]

Storage methods

Proper refrigeration technology is used to keep sweet potatoes for long periods of time [Karuri, E.G. and Ojijo, N.K.O. 1994]. Some of the common storage methods that are used for small scale production include in ground, pit, clamp, and indoor storage and all extend the storage time of sweet potatoes by some degree [Dandago MA, and Gungula DT, 2011].

Small scale production storage methods.

In-ground. Sweet potatoes are commonly left in the ground and eaten or sold directly following harvest, this is called piece-meal or sequential harvesting [Karuri, E.G. and Hagenimana, V. 1995]. In-ground storage is used to protect the tubers while reducing the work required to set up storage facilities [Windmill, 2014].

Pit storage. Involves digging a hole in the ground for storing the potatoes, it differs from in-ground as tubers are collected and kept together and considerations are made to control the storage environment. Construction materials commonly used are; grass, soil, wood, lime, sawdust and ash [Mutandwa E, and Gadzirayi CT. 2007].

Flamed grass [pest free] is used to line the bottom and sides of the pit for insulation against temperature change and absorb moisture [Devereau AD, 1994]. Soil as a filler and roof sealant were as wood and plant material can be used to strengthen walls as well as to create roof covering [keeps rain out and provide shade to lower temperatures]. Lime is used to absorbing CO_2 while sawdust is used as a cushioning material and controls condensation on the tubers. Wood ash can be applied to potatoes prior to storage and protects against insect attacks and mould [Mutandwa E, and Gadzirayi CT. 2007].

To promote drainage the pit should ideally be dug into a sloppy ground. It should be at least 0.35 m above the water table during dry and wet seasons and be approximately 0.5 m below the surface [Devereau AD, 1994]. As commonly the pit will be sealed shut in order to maintain a good RH but CO_2 will collect and cause spoilage. To minimise ventilation problems, a sizable headspace should be maintained in the pit to help promote airflow. Pits can be reused but they should be cleaned, the soil turned over and disinfected with fire or sulphur to rid the area of any microorganisms. Losses are still fairly high for this technique, though it has been shown in some instances to keep roots for 2–4 months [Mutandwa E, and Gadzirayi CT. 2007].

Clamp and mound storage. Consists of covered piles of sweet potatoes, stacked in a heap on a layer of grass and covered in layers of grass and soil. Ash, lime and sawdust can be used for added effect. Piles can be made at ground level or in shallow or deep trenches. Drainage should be considered and ruts may be made in the ground to lead off water. Clamps may be covered by a roof or kept in a building for added protection. To minimise losses due to respiration a ventilation shaft can be added. Estimated storage time is 2-3 months [Devereau AD, 1994].

Indoor storage. Stored in buildings [living area or in a granary]. In home storage can be done in straw woven baskets, cloth bags or wooden boxes. Baskets and boxes are more effective as they minimise mechanical damage. Tubers should be kept off the ground to keep away from rodents and other pests. Indoor storage is an effective technique for maintaining proper ventilation though depending on the type of building maintaining proper storage temperature and RH may be difficult [Devereau AD, 1994]. Granaries or other storage buildings typically consist of a round hut with walls made of straw, mud, clay and wood and a conical straw roof. These are commonly supported above ground by a system of legs to keep the crop dry and away from animals, rodents and pests [Dandago MA, and Gungula DT. 2011].

Large scale production storage

After curing, sweet potatoes may be stored for 4 to 7 months under proper conditions, including ventilation. Sweet potatoes are cleaned, either by brushing or washing, and then sometimes waxed before packing into boxes, crates or baskets for market [Kaiser & Ernst, 2014]. According to Devereau AD [1994], optimum storage of sweet potatoes occurs at 12–16 °C, 85–90% relative humidity [RH] but requires proper ventilation to remove excess CO_2 [CO_2 increases the spoilage rate] and bring in oxygen [O_2] for respiration. Some of the spoilage factors are highlighted in Figure 5.

Diseases and damages in storage

Diseases and other defects can be of field or storage origin. The best precautions are careful control of curing and storage conditions, and good sanitation procedures. Roots cured immediately after harvest under proper conditions and harvested during good field conditions with minimum harvest injury nearly always give fewer problems and less storage loss than poorly handled roots [WFLO, 2008]. Revealed that curing sweet potato roots by cutting off vines 4-5 days prior to harvest reduced rotting by 17% [CGIAR, 2016].

The sweet potato weevil [*Cylas formicarius [F.](Coleoptera: Brentidae)]* is a serious field and storage insect pest, where no adequate control is available and therefore infested roots should not be stored. Roots should not be shipped from weevil infested production sites to other areas of the country. Fruit flies [*Drosophila spp.*] and soldier flies [*Hermetia illucens (Diptera: Stratiomyidae)*] can be problems when there are diseased, soured or damaged roots in storage, but both can be controlled with sanitation and/or appropriate insecticide treatment. Viruses and the sweet potato weevil are serious quarantine issues. Viral diseases are of concern if roots are used for propagation material.

Table 5: Diseases and controls [WFLO, 2008]

DISEASE	DESCRIPTION	CONTROL
Black Rot	Of field origin. Circular brown, slightly sunken superficial spots initially, enlarging to black or greenish-black areas, ½ to 2 inches, possibly appearing rough with tiny bristles. Diseased tissues are firm and bitter tasting. Non-diseased tissue also bitter when cooked.	Disinfection of seed roots. Propagation with vine or bed cuttings. Keep stock from diseased fields separate. Market sweet potatoes from infected fields promptly. Careful handling to avoid wounding. Washing or waxing potatoes may spread disease. Treatment of roots with a registered effective fungicide and sanitizing grading equipment between lots can greatly reduce losses.
Charcoal Rot	Initially irregular-shaped, light brown discoloration with sharp line of demarcation between diseased and sound tissues. Later, dark brown and firm, the skin shrivelling. Final stage shows a hard, dry, charcoal-like mummy. Three distinct colour zones in diseased tissues when potato is cut. Disease progresses slowly in storage.	Do not store, ship or use as seed any potatoes showing slightest decay at tips. Curing helps control decay through cork formation in injuries.
Dry Rot	First dark brown and firm, usually at end of potato; later becoming withered black and hard. Surface of diseased areas seems covered with black pimples. Develops in storage.	No definite control method except in seed stock selection.
Surface and End Rot	A considerable variety of rots with firm dry tissues, initially small, circular, light brown, superficial spots and withering of ends of potatoes. Invasion occurs through wounds and through tissue broken down by other organisms. Decay develops slowly, shrivelling follows severe infection	Careful handling to avoid wounding of tissues especially tips. Prompt curing under optimal temperature and humidity conditions to promote rapid healing of wounds made during harvest. Where possible, avoid wet-weather harvest.
Foot Rot	Firm to spongy dark brown, especially at attached end of potato. Resembles black rot, but is not bristly.	Potatoes showing evident decay should not be stored or shipped to distant markets, or used in seed stock selection.
Internal Cork	A virus disease that causes the development of dark brown to blackish corky spots in the flesh which vary in size and shape and may occur singly or in groups. Some spotted roots may be found when dug, but the problem may show a considerable increase after 4-6 months storage.	Proper storage at 13 to 16°C. Avoid storage at 21°C or above. Use resistant cultivars or varieties. Sweet potatoes suspected of being infected with internal cork should be marketed soon after harvest.
Java Black Rot	Initially brown and moderately firm, turning to black and firm with pimply surface. Eventually dry black mummy. Develops slowly in transit or storage only after harvest.	Careful handling and proper curing.
Rhizopus Soft Rot	A very destructive and rapid developing transit and storage rot, evidenced by a soft and watery appearance with a yeasty odour. Later tissues become cinnamon-brown to light chocolate colour, but never black. Final stage a hard brown mummy. Coarse, stringy "whiskers" with white and black spore balls are often characteristic. Wet soil increases this decay.	Careful handling and prompt curing at harvest. Treat crowded roots with Botran or other recommended fungicides before shipment, especially those coming out of storage.
Scurf	Very common, causing skin-deep small greyish spots and blotches, later merging into brown areas. Spots often occur in field, but may enlarge in storage. Unless extensive, usually overlooked by trade. Does not grow on plant parts above ground.	Disinfect seed roots. Propagate by vine or bed cuttings.
Soil Rot [Pox]	Soil rot of field origin causes dry, brown pits or pox Marks, of irregular size and shape, ¼ to 1 inch in diameter, on root surface spots. May become rough with irregular margin as they mature, always firm and dry not followed by other decay. Most serious during dry seasons.	Do not use as seed any potatoes showing symptoms. Plant in disease-free soils, if possible; 7-9 year rotation reduces problem if severe. Also addition of sulphur to make soil acidic [pH 5.0] reduces incidence.

Preparation for Market

Because of the changes in pectin and starch levels which occur during curing and storage, uncured roots are often preferred for canning and some frozen products, since uncured roots produce a firmer product. The better flavour and texture of cured and stored sweet potatoes is evident in pureed products, including baby food, dehydrated flakes, and some frozen products. Sweet potatoes stored for such uses should be held in the same conditions as those stored for marketing as fresh roots [WFLO, 2008].

Grading

Careful grading, cleaning, and packing of sweet potatoes and putting them on the market when there is a good demand means better prices. The market demands uniform medium-sized sweet potatoes, free from bruises or decayed spots. In grading those that are too large or too small, as well as those that are misshapen, cut, or bruised, should be used for making stock feed or for canning. After being carefully graded, the sweet potatoes should be put into clean, attractive packages. An attractive pack of well-graded sweet potatoes will usually bring a better price than an ungraded one [Sumner P.E. 1984].

Sweet potatoes are graded into U.S. Extra No. 1, U.S. No. 1, U.S. Commercial, U.S. No. 2, and Unclassified based largely on size, condition, and absence of defects. Desired sizes are 8.3 to 8.9 cm in diameter and 0.53 to 0.59 kg. During storage in the U.S., roots are commonly handled in 360 kg bulk bins but are generally marketed in 18 kg boxes, but at the retail level, roots are typically displayed loose unrefrigerated, at about 21°C [WFLO, 2008].

Washing

Wash both the newly harvested and the cured sweet potatoes before they are packaged for market. When black rot is present, washing seriously spreads the disease particularly in the freshly harvested crop; however, the sweet potatoes are still washed because of market demands for an attractive product. Washing should not be more extensive than necessary to remove the soil. Care should be taken not to make fresh wounds such as broken ends because of the danger that soft rot organisms may infect them [Sumner P.E. 1984].

Sweet potatoes are usually removed from storage, washed and re-graded prior to marketing. This results in a product which from a storage standpoint is similar to uncured roots. During the grading process the roots are often treated with a fungicide to reduce rot incidence and lightly waxed to limit moisture loss. Washed and graded roots should be kept at high humidity and at temperatures above chilling and moved through marketing channels as quickly as possible. Shelf life of washed and fungicide-treated roots is only 2-3 weeks [WFLO, 2008].

Shelf Life

Washed and graded roots should be kept at high humidity and at temperatures above chilling and moved through marketing channels as quickly as possible. Shelf life of washed and fungicide-treated roots is only 2-3 weeks [WFLO, 2008].

Household level [Freezing]

To avoid browning discoloration, peeled, sliced or diced sweet potatoes should be blanched in such a manner that they are heated to a centre temperature of 88°C as rapidly as practicable. Following such treatment, they can be frozen satisfactorily as such, or after further cooking. Much of the commercial pack is sugar glazed, although the potatoes can be mashed, pureed, baked or just sliced and packed as such, or as a component of frozen food dinners or canned soup. Cooked and glazed sweet potatoes retain a satisfactory shelf life at -18°C for 8 months. If not thoroughly cooked or unglazed, shelf life may be limited to 4-6 months [WFLO, 2008]. Roots intended for canning or freezing may be held without curing at 2-4.4 °C up to 10 days. However, roots held at field temperatures for only 3 to 4 days will result in a decrease in firmness of the processed product.

References

AREX. 2004. Ministry of Lands and Agriculture, Department of Agricultural Research and Extension. An overview of Zimbabwe's' agriculture. Harare, Zimbabwe: Author.

Bradley A. King and Jeffrey C. Stark, 1997. Potato irrigation management.

CGIAR. 2016. Expanding utilization of RTB crops and reducing their post-harvest losses. Proposed Business Case Improving the shelf life of harvested sweet potato roots in the market and household level.

Cheryl Kaiser and Matt Ernst. 2014. Sweet Potato. University of Kentucky College of Agriculture, Food and Environment. Center for Crop Diversifcaton Crop Profle.

Dandago MA, and Gungula DT. 2011. Effects of various storage methods on the quality and nutritional composition of sweet potato (Ipomea batatas L.) in Yola Nigeria. International Food Research Journal 18:271-278

Dandago MA, and Gungula DT. 2011. Effects of various storage methods on the quality and nutritional composition of sweet potato [Ipomea batatas L.] in Yola Nigeria. International Food Research Journal 18:271-278

Devereau AD. 1994. Tropical sweet potato storage: A literature review. Report. Natural Resources Institute, Chatham

Dukuh, I. G. *et al*, 2015. Developing Technology to Improve the Shelf Life of Sweet Potato Tubers. Available online at www.ijpab.com.

Ewell, P. 1993. Sweet potato in Africa: Research priorities to stimulate increased marketing. Paper presented at the International Workshop on Methods for Agricultural Marketing Research, 16–20 March 1993, IARI Campus, New Delhi, India

FAO, nd. Farm Management Handbook Volume 1. Field Crop Production

Filippone P.T. 2017. Sweet Potato Selection and Storage. The Spruce. Accessed 28 January 2018.

Fritz VA. 2012. Plastic Mulches: Benefits, Types, and Sources. Minnesota High Tunnel Production Manual for Commercial Growers – Second Edition. http://hightunnels.cfans.umn.edu

Hall AJ and Devereau D. 2000. Low-cost storage of fresh sweet potatoes in Uganda: Lessons from participatory and on-station approaches to technology choice and adaptive testing. Outlook on Agriculture. 29(4):275-282

Horticultural Research Institute. http://www.drss.gov.zw. Accessed 6/29/2016.

Kapinga RE *et al*, 2003. Increasing the contribution of sweet potato to sustainable rural livelihoods in Tanzania. Proceedings of the Twelfth Symposium of The International Society for Tropical Root Crops: Potential of Root Crops for Food and Industrial Resources, Tsuk, pp. 285-291

Karuri, E.G. and Hagenimana, V. 1995). Use of ambient conditions and sawdust in storage of sweet potato [Ipomoea batatas L.] roots in Kenya. Zimbabwe Journal of Agricultural Research. 33(1):83-91

Karuri, E.G. and Ojijo, N.K.O. 1994. Storage studies on sweet potato roots: Experiences with KSP20 cultivar. Acta Horticulture 368: 441-452

Lamont W, 2014. Growing Potatoes Using Plasticulture. Penn State Extension. http://agsci.psu.edu. Accessed 6/29/2016

M. A. Badr · S. D. Abou Hussein · W. A. El-Tohamy ·N. Gruda. 2010. Effciency of Subsurface Drip Irrigation for Potato Production Under Different Dry Stress Conditions. Springer-Verlag 2010. Available at https://www.researchgate.net/publication/227215403. Accessed March 16, 2016.

Mutandwa E, and Gadzirayi CT. 2007. Comparative assessment of indigenous methods of sweet potato preservation among smallholder farmers: Case of grass, ash and soil based approaches in Zimbabwe. African Studies Quarterly 9, no. 3: [online] URL:http://web.africa.ufl.edu/asq/v9/v9i3a4.htm.

Mutandwa. 2008. Performance of Tissue-Cultured Sweet Potatoes Among Smallholder Farmers in Zimbabwe *AgBioForum, 11(1): 48-57. ©2008 AgBioForum.*

NCSPC, 2018. Sweet Potatoes Keep You Moving. Available at www.ncsweetpotato.com Accessed 28 Jan 2018

NDJ. 2014. © 2014 NaanDanJain Ltd. All rights reserved.

New England Vegetable Guide, nd. https://nevegetable.org. Accessed on 3/16/2016

New Farmer Zimbabwe. 2014. Sweet Potato Production. Accessed on 07 March 2018. Available online https://www.facebook.com/newfarmerzimbabwe/.

Parwada et al, 2011. Effect of ridge height and planting orientation on Ipomea batatas (sweet potato) production. Journal of Agricultural Biotechnology and Sustainable Development Vol. 3(4) pp. 72-76, April 2011. Available online http://www.academicjournals.org/JABSD

Patel N, Rajput TBS. 2008. Dynamics and modelling of soil water under subsurface drip irrigated onion. Agric Water Manag 95:1335–1349.

Patel N, Rajput TBS. 2007. Effect of drip tape placement depth and irrigation level on yield of potato. Agric Water Manag 88:209–223

Ramirez P. 1992. Cultivation harvesting and storage of sweet potato products. In: Roots, tubers, plantains and bananas in animal feeding. (Eds Machin, D.; Nyvold, S.), Proceedings of the F AO Expert Consultation held in CIAT, Cali, Colombia 21–25 January 1991; FAO Animal Production and Health Paper – 95

Rukuni, M., & Eicher, C. 2006. Zimbabwe's agricultural revolution [2nd Ed.]. Harare, Zimbabwe: University of Zimbabwe.

Sanders D, 2001. Using Plastic Mulches and Drip Irrigation for Vegetables. http://content.ces.ncsu.edu Accessed on March 16, 2016

Sanginga, N, 2015. Root and Tuber Crops (Cassava, Yam, Potato and Sweet Potato). Feeding Africa.

Shock CC. *et al,* 2013. Drip Irrigation Guide for Potatoes. Accessed 28 January 2018. Available at https://catalog.extension.oregonstate.edu/em8912

Sumner P.E. 1984. Harvesting, Curing And Storage Of Sweet Potatoes. Cooperative Extension Service The University Of Georgia College Of Agriculture

The Toro Company, 2010. Crop Solutions. Drip Irrigation on Potatoes. toromicroirrigation.com

WFLO, 2008. Sweet Potatoes. WFLO Commodity Storage Manual.

Windmill, 2014. Production requirements & costs for 1 ha of Sweet Potatoes [1 hectare - 2.47 acres].

Appendices

Appendices A: Zimbabwe -Agro-ecological Zones Map [OCHA, 2009].

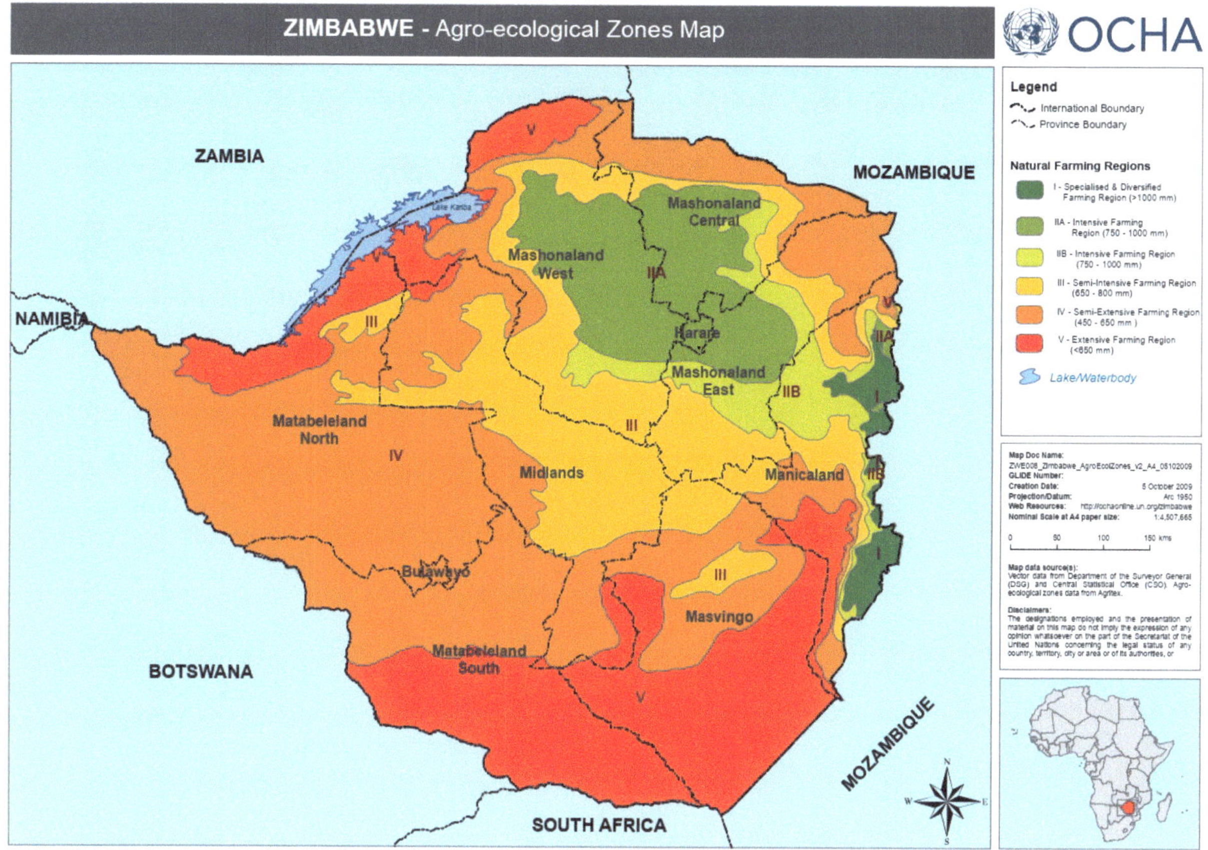

Appendices B: Monthly ETo Penman-Monteith Data.

```
                    MONTHLY ETO PENMAN-MONTEITH DATA
     (File: C:\Program Files (x86)\CLIMWAT 2.0 for CROPWAT V2.0\HERNDERSON.pen)


     Country: Location 15              Station: HERNDERSON
     Altitude: 1290 m.                 Latitude: 17.58 °S      Longitude: 30.96 °E
```

Month	Min Temp °C	Max Temp °C	Humidity %	Wind km/day	Sun hours	Rad MJ/m²/day	ETo mm/day
January	16.1	26.7	78	121	6.0	20.0	4.10
February	16.0	26.5	80	104	6.1	19.7	3.95
March	14.0	26.9	74	104	7.3	20.4	4.04
April	11.3	26.4	71	104	7.7	18.7	3.62
May	6.8	24.6	66	104	8.2	17.1	3.10
June	3.9	22.6	63	112	8.0	15.6	2.72
July	2.8	22.7	57	121	8.0	16.1	2.87
August	4.5	25.0	52	138	8.6	18.9	3.66
September	7.5	28.0	46	164	8.9	21.8	4.79
October	11.6	30.1	49	173	8.6	23.0	5.46
November	14.5	28.3	63	156	6.7	20.9	4.75
December	15.9	26.9	74	138	6.0	19.9	4.22
Average	10.4	26.2	64	128	7.5	19.3	3.94

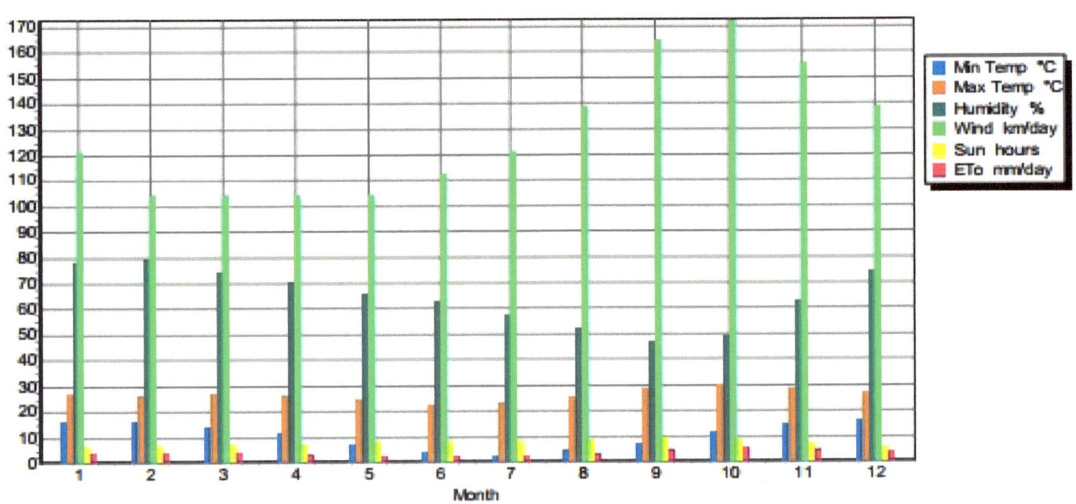

Appendices C: Monthly Rain Data

```
                        MONTHLY RAIN DATA
      (File: C:\Program Files (x86)\CLIMWAT 2.0 for CROPWAT V2.0\HERNDERSON.cli)


Station: HERNDERSON

Eff. rain method: USDA Soil Conservation Service formula:
                  Peff = Pmon * (125 - 0.2 * Pmon) / 125   for Pmon <= 250 mm
                  Peff = 125 + 0.1 * Pmon                  for Pmon  > 250 mm


                  Rain      Eff rain
                   mm          mm

January          209.0       139.1
February         175.0       126.0
March            121.0        97.6
April             43.0        40.0
May               17.0        16.5
June               2.0         2.0
July               2.0         2.0
August             2.0         2.0
September          5.0         5.0
October           32.0        30.4
November          99.0        83.3
December         187.0       131.0

Total            894.0       674.9
```

Appendices D: Dry crop Data -Potato

```
                        DRY CROP DATA
        (File: C:\ProgramData\CROPWAT\data\crops\FAO\POTATO.CRO)


Crop Name:  Potato                Planting date: 15/11    Harvest: 24/03

Stage             initial     develop       mid        late       total

Length (days)       25          30          45          30         130
Kc Values          0.50        -->         1.15        0.75
Rooting depth (m)  0.30        -->         0.60        0.60
Critical depletion 0.25        -->         0.30        0.50
Yield response f.  0.45        0.80        0.80        0.30        1.10
Cropheight (m)                             0.60
```

Appendices E: Soil Data -Red sandy Loam

```
                        SOIL DATA
     (File: C:\ProgramData\CROPWAT\data\soils\RED SANDY LOAM.SOI)


Soil name: RED SANDY LOAM

General soil data:

    Total available soil moisture (FC - WP)     140.0    mm/meter
    Maximum rain infiltration rate                 30    mm/day
    Maximum rooting depth                         900    centimeters
    Initial soil moisture depletion (as % TA      50    %
    Initial available soil moisture             70.0    mm/meter
```

Appendices F: Crop Water Requirements [CWR]

```
                    CROP WATER REQUIREMENTS


ETo station: HERNDERSON              Crop: Potato
Rain station: HERNDERSON             Planting date: 15/11
```

Month	Decade	Stage	Kc coeff	ETc mm/day	ETc mm/dec	Eff rain mm/dec	Irr. Req. mm/dec
Nov	2	Init	0.50	2.38	14.3	16.8	0.3
Nov	3	Init	0.50	2.29	22.9	33.2	0.0
Dec	1	Deve	0.50	2.21	22.1	39.6	0.0
Dec	2	Deve	0.63	2.67	26.7	45.5	0.0
Dec	3	Deve	0.85	3.54	39.0	45.8	0.0
Jan	1	Mid	1.06	4.37	43.7	46.1	0.0
Jan	2	Mid	1.11	4.57	45.7	47.3	0.0
Jan	3	Mid	1.11	4.51	49.6	45.5	4.1
Feb	1	Mid	1.11	4.46	44.6	43.9	0.6
Feb	2	Mid	1.11	4.40	44.0	42.7	1.3
Feb	3	Late	1.08	4.30	34.4	39.3	0.0
Mar	1	Late	0.97	3.87	38.7	36.6	2.1
Mar	2	Late	0.84	3.38	33.8	33.9	0.0
Mar	3	Late	0.75	2.91	11.6	9.8	0.0
					471.0	526.1	8.4

CROP IRRIGATION SCHEDULE

ETo station: **HERNDERSON**   Crop: Potato   Planting date: 15/11
Rain station: **HERNDERSON**   Soil: RED SANDY LOAM   Harvest date: 24/03

Yield red.:   0.2 %

Crop scheduling options
    Timing: Irrigate at 100 % depletion
    Application: Refill to 100 % of field capacity
    Field eff.   70 %

Table format: Irrigation schedule

Date	Day	Stage	Rain mm	Ks fract.	Eta %	Depl %	Net mm	IrrDeficit mm	Loss mm	Gr. Irr mm	Flow l/s/h
15 Nov	1	Init	0.0	0.67	67	54	23.0	0.0	0.0	32.8	3.80
21 Nov	7	Init	0.0	1.00	100	26	12.5	0.0	0.0	17.8	0.34
2 Jan	49	Dev	0.0	1.00	100	33	26.5	0.0	0.0	37.8	0.10
12 Jan	59	Mid	0.0	1.00	100	32	26.6	0.0	0.0	38.0	0.44
22 Jan	69	Mid	0.0	1.00	100	32	27.3	0.0	0.0	39.0	0.45
1 Feb	79	Mid	0.0	1.00	100	32	27.0	0.0	0.0	38.6	0.45
12 Feb	90	Mid	0.0	1.00	100	32	26.6	0.0	0.0	38.0	0.40
22 Feb	100	Mid	0.0	1.00	100	31	26.2	0.0	0.0	37.4	0.43
24 Mar	End	End	0.0	1.00	0	7					

Totals:

Total gross irrigation	279.5 mm	Total rainfall	733.6
Total net irrigation	195.7 mm	Effective rainfall	307.6
Total irrigation losses	0.0 mm	Total rain loss	426.0
Actual water use by crop	467.3 mm	Moist deficit at harvest	6.0
Potential water use by crop	468.1 mm	Actual irrigation requirement	160.5
Efficiency irrigation schedule 100.0 %		Efficiency rain	41.9
Deficiency irrigation schedule 0.2 %			

Yield reductions:

Stagelabel	A	B	C	D	Season
Reductions in ETc	1.4	0.0	0.0	0.0	0.2
Yield response factor	0.45	0.80	0.80	0.30	1.10
Yield reduction	0.6	0.0	0.0	0.0	0.2
Cumulative yield reduction	0.6	0.6	0.6	0.6